I0472368

THE SMALL ENTREPRENEUR

SECRETS TO SMALL BUSINESS SUCCESS

ELVIS LANGHA, CPA

Disclaimer

The Small Entrepreneur

Copyrights Reserved © 2019- Elvis Langha

DEDICATION

To My Mom, Vasti
You sowed, but unfortunately never reaped. I wouldn't be half the man I am today if it wasn't for you

Foreword

Most entrepreneurs are aware that the efforts required to turn an idea, product, or service into a groundbreaking and continuous success is nothing short of herculean.

The steps involved in this process are countless and highly complex. From refining the initial concept, defining the target market, developing an all-encompassing business plan, conducting in-depth market research, successfully selling the program to potential investors, to lining up vendors, suppliers, and partners. All of this takes place before you have even determined the type of staffing requirements you might face down the road.

So, what makes a successful entrepreneur and a winning business concept? It comes down to some principles that most entrepreneurs agree are central to every startup effort: passion for your idea, ability to communicate well, enthusiasm for research, and concern for the overall consumer experience.

The best startups are born from a strong belief or concept, which is held passionately by the "entrepreneur in charge." If you want to drive your business forward, you should have the correct motivation along with the proper sense of purpose in what you are doing.

It starts with launching and sustaining your mission, having a succinct vision, and developing an authoritative mission statement. Even though it is a foundation for all your marketing efforts, your mission statement is also a launchpad which can be used for effectively communicating with investors as well as partners. If you do not prepare a business plan or cannot concisely explain what your business does, you will have immense difficulty getting anyone to listen to you.

Advances in logistics and technology (think e-commerce) have shifted the paradigm, and successful entrepreneurs understand that their potential marketplace is the entire world. Through this book, I aim to shed light on some of the most important strategies that small companies should embrace to achieve success.

I hope this roadmap helps your startup move on the path to ultimate success as you avoid the bumps others before you have face.

Table of Content

Chapter 1: Small Businesses at Glance

"The Journey of a thousand miles begins with a step." Lao Tzu (Chinese Philosopher)

Depending on the industry you are operating in, a small business could be defined as any business with a maximum of 1,500 employees. Small businesses are privately owned partnerships, sole proprietorships, or companies which generate less revenue than large businesses.

Small businesses are important for our economy. However, what exactly do these small businesses look like? The government or more specifically, the Small Business Administration (SBA), help answer all these questions.

What Defines a Small Business?

The SBA has set numerical definitions, or "size standards" for all the small businesses operating in the United States. This quantitative definition is based on the number of employees and the average annual receipts of the business.

However, these standard sizes are not one size fits all. Instead, the definition of a small business depends on the type of industry the business is operating in. Depending on the industry, a small business could be defined as either a maximum of 250 employees or a maximum of 1,500 employees, which may not seem like such a "small" business, at least to a solo entrepreneur.

Main Characteristics of a Small Business

Not every small business ultimately grows to the size of a large company. Some companies are ideally suited to operate on a small scale for several years, often serving a local community and producing just enough profit to take care of the company owners. Small-scale businesses exhibit a distinct set of classifying characteristics that set them apart from their larger counterparts.

Fewer Locations

A small-scale business, by definition, can be found only in a limited area. These businesses are not likely to have sales outlets in several states or countries. Many small-scale businesses function from a single office, retail store or service outlet. It is even possible to run a small business directly out of your home, without any business facilities.

Small Market Area

Small-scale businesses serve a much smaller geographical area than companies or larger private businesses. The smallest scale businesses serve a single community, for example, a convenience store in a township. The very characterization of small-scale prevents these corporations from serving areas much larger than a local area, as growing beyond that would increase the scale of a small business's operations and push it into a new classification.

Few Employees

Small-scale businesses employ smaller teams of workers than corporations that operate on larger scales. The smallest businesses are run individually by single entities or small teams. A larger small-scale business can every so often employ fewer than one hundred employees, depending on the nature of the business operations

Sole or Partnership Ownership and Taxes

The corporate form (C Corporation) of business might not well be suited to small-scale operations. Instead, small-scale businesses prefer to organize as sole proprietorships, partnerships, limited liability companies, or S Corporations (more about that later). These forms of organization provide the greatest degree of administrative control for company owners while minimizing the hassle and expenditure of business registration. These businesses usually do not file their own taxes; instead, company owners report business income and expenses on their personal tax returns.

Misconceptions about Small Businesses

You often hear that more than half of new small businesses fail within the first year of their inception. According to the SBA, this is not necessarily true. The SBA quantifies that only 30% of new businesses fail during the first two years, and more than 50% fail during their first five years. The SBA also states that only 25% of these small businesses make it beyond fifteen years. These small businesses can avert their rates of failure through proper planning, funding, and flexibility.

"Goals. There's no telling what you can do when you get inspired by them. There's no telling what you can do when you believe in them. There's no telling what will happen when you act upon them." Jim Rohn (American Entrepreneur)

There is common hope shared by many small business owners: you hope to hire and foster motivated workers who are productive, who exceed your expectations, and who actively look for ways to improve your product or service offerings. When they need a little "push," an extra incentive, such as offering fringe benefits such as health insurance, paid time off (PTO), and/or retirement benefits helps differentiate your business from competitors. Multiple ways of finding quality and talented team members abound (https://www.topechelon.com/blog/recruiter-train- ing/sources-recruitment-types/). These include but are not limited to:

Online Job Boards: These range from generic to industry-specific job boards where an employer can post job openings for interested candidates actively seeking employment. It's worth noting that this service comes with a fee and should be incorporated when preparing your annual budget.

- **Social Media:** Imagine how many people have Facebook, Twitter, Instagram and LinkedIn accounts. As you are undoubtedly aware, the best source of candidates is sometimes peer referral. Using social media to attract candidates is a great source of tapping into your existing workforce's network. Conversely, some sites may not provide enough insight into a candidate's skillset.

- **Competitors:** This can be a goldmine since competitors sometimes have staff members seeking to make a career move for the right reasons. However, it is advisable to inquire about potential non-compete agreements prior to setting up interviews.

- **Networking Events:** A myriad of local networking events is held regularly. Sites like Eventbrite are a good source of finding these events based on your interest and industry. Generally, these events are an opportunity to informally interview your prospects and discern if they will be a good fit for the open position. The major flip side of this approach is the "love at first sight" syndrome whereby you can be interested in someone's skills only to find out they are satisfied with their current employment.

For employers and employees alike, there is nothing better than earning money from what one is most passionate about. However, remember money, as you might have discovered, is not always "the magic motivator" that will set employees' determination on fire. As it turns out, goal-setting is the first step toward eliciting greater productivity, commitment, and dedication from employees.

This is hardly a fresh or revolutionary theory. Edwin Locke came up with this idea in his article *Toward a Theory of Task Motivation and Incentives* (Locke, 1968). Like any practical small business owner who knows a thing or two about motivational strategies, Locke saw a direct relationship between setting goals and completing tasks, provided that the company goals are definite and challenging.

Locke's goal-setting theory of motivation has survived the test of time, with today's management experts modernizing it with a handy abbreviation: SMART. Goals should be specific, measurable, attainable, relevant and time-bound. As a smart small business owner, you know it is a good idea to recognize the advantages and possible limitations of goal-setting and how SMART can help you strengthen one priority while minimizing another.

Goal Setting Takes Root Early

Setting goals for your business may begin with a "eureka" moment of inspiration or with a long, thought-out process. Like numerous business owners, the goal-setting approach may have taken root early, before they even realized it. Parents, teachers, and others may have encouraged this mindset without necessarily using the word "goal" in questions such as:

"What do you want to be when you grow up? Where would you like to go to college? What will you major in?"

And later, as the idea of entrepreneurship captures your imagination:

"What type of business can you see yourself managing? How will you distinguish yourself from the competition? What does your five-year plan look like?"

The intention in questions like these is clear: setting goals is very important. It is the sign of a motivated, disciplined individual. Similarly, someone who insists on "living in the moment," with little thought about next year or the year after that, is perhaps not capable of managing a small business. You don't have to be a visionary, but forward-thinking reaps numerous dividends if you have ambitions for your smallbusiness.

Goal Setting Theory

Management experts and theorists tout the importance of motivation and goal-setting for businesses. So do psychology experts. According to a Florida State University report:

"In psychology, the research on goal-setting has a long tradition. Studies have consistently demonstrated that an individual's behavior is affected by goals and that, if well chosen; goals can boost individual productivity." (https://wol.iza.org/articles/goal-setting-and-worker-motivation/long)

Locke's theory has been tested and analyzed so many times that it is practically viewed as conventional wisdom. According to a research study at the University of Minnesota:

"The theory has been supported in over 1,000 studies with employees ranging from blue-collar workers to research and development employees, and there is strong support that setting goals are related to performance improvements." (http://jbep-net.com/journals/Vol_3_No_1_March_2016/8.pdf)

The clearly established connection between goal-setting and motivation has been embraced by more than just small business owners. Some of the biggest names in the corporate and tech world use the goal-setting theory to stimulate employee action.

Goal Setting Theory by Locke

Goal-setting theory (Locke & Latham, 1990) is one of the most influential and practical theories of motivation. In fact, in a survey of organizational behavior scholars, it has been rated as the most important [out of 73 theories] (Miner, 2003). The theory has been supported in over 1,000 studies with employees ranging from blue-collar workers to re-search and development employees, and there is strong support that setting goals is related to performance im-provements (Ivancevich & McMahon, 1982; Latham & Locke, 2006; Umstot, Bell, & Mitchell, 1976). Ac-cording to one estimate, goal setting improves performance at least 10%–25% (Pritchard et al., 1988).

Setting SMART Goals

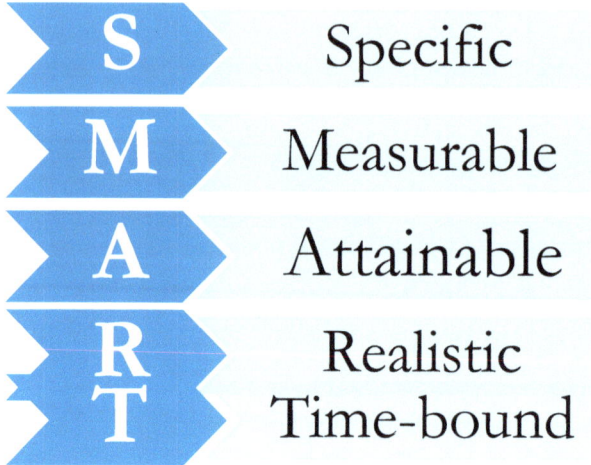

As essential as goals are, their mere presence does not necessarily motivate workers of your small business. Think about New Year's resolutions that you made but failed to keep. Perhaps you decided that you would lose some weight over the year, but then never put a solid plan into action. Or maybe you decided that you would read more but did not. Why did your goal fail? Research evidence has indicated that effective goals are SMART. A SMART goal is a goal that is specific, measurable, attainable, realistic, and time-bound.

Specific
Effective goals are specific and measurable. For instance, "increasing sales to a region by 30%" is a specific goal, while deciding to "delight clients" is neither specific nor measurable. When the goals you set are specific, performance tends to be higher (Tubbs, 1986) (http://psycnet.apa.org/record/1986-29994-001). Why? If goals are not specific and measurable, how would you know whether you have reached the goal? A wide distribution of performance levels could potentially be acceptable. For the same reason, "doing your best" is not

an effective goal, because it is not measurable and does not give you a specific target

Measurable

Certain aspects of performance are easier to quantify. For example, it is relatively easy to set specific goals for productivity, sales, number of defects, or turnover rates. However, not everything that is easy to measure should be measured. Moreover, some of the most important elements of someone's performance may not be easily quantifiable (such as employee or customer satisfaction).

So, how do you set specific and measurable goals for these soft targets? Even though some effort will be involved, metrics such as satisfaction can and should be quantified. For example, you could design a survey for employees and customers to track satisfaction ratings from year to year. Alternatively, consumers could post reviews online to rate the company's products and services.

Aggressive but Attainable

Effective goals are difficult, not easy. Aggressive but attainable goals are also called stretch goals. According to a Hay Group study, one factor that distinguishes companies that are ranked as "Most Admired Companies" in Fortune 500 magazine (http://fortune.com/) is that they set more difficult goals (Stein, 2000). People with difficult goals outperform those with easier goals (Mento, Steel, & Karren, 1987; Phillips & Gully, 1997; Tubbs, 1986; Yukl & Latham, 1978). Why? Easy goals do not provide a challenge. When goals are aggressive and require people to work harder or smarter, performance tends to be dramatically higher. Research shows that people who have a high level of self-efficacy and people who have a high need for achievement tend to set more difficult goals for themselves (Phillips & Gully, 1997).

Realistic

While goals should be difficult, they should also be based on reality. In other words, if a goal is viewed as impossible to reach, it will not have any motivational value. In fact, setting impossible goals and then penalizing people for not reaching these goals is unkind and will demoralize employees.

Time-Bound

The goal should contain a statement regarding when the proposed performance level will be reached. For example, "increasing sales to a region by 10%" is not a time-bound goal because there is no time limit. Adding a limiter such as "by December of the current fiscal year" gives employees a sense of urgency

Here is an example of a SMART goal: Wal-Mart Stores Inc. recently set a goal to eliminate 25% of the solid waste from U.S. stores by the year 2019. This goal meets all the conditions of being SMART (if 25% is a difficult yet realistic goal). Even though it seems like a simple concept, numerous goals that are set within organizations might not be SMART.

How Do SMART Goals Motivate?

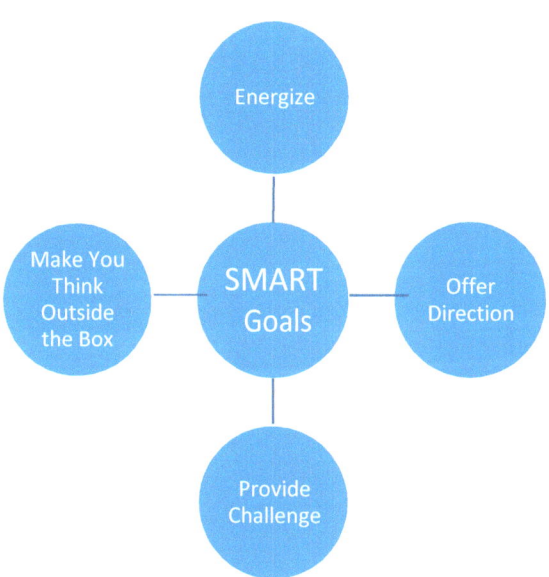

There are at least four reasons why goals motivate. Firstly, goals give direction. The goal tells you what to focus on. For this reason, goals should be set carefully. To avoid any potential conflicts of interest, employees must understand and accept the company's vision and mission.

Secondly, goals energize people and tell them not to stop until the goal is accomplished. If you set goals for yourself such as "I will take a snack break from reading this textbook when I finish reading this section," you will likely not give up until you reach the end of the section. Even if you feel tired along the way, having this specific goal will urge you to move forward.

Thirdly, having a goal provides a challenge. When people have goals and achieve them, they feel a sense of accomplishment.

Finally, SMART goals urge people to think outside the box and re-think how they are working. If the goal is not very difficult, it only motivates people to work faster or longer. If a goal is substantially difficult, merely working faster or longer will not get you the results. Instead, you will need to reinvent the process and devise a creative way of working. Having a goal that went beyond the speed capabilities of traditional trains prevented engineers from making minor improvements and inspired them to come up with a radically different concept as illustrated in the following graphic (Kerr & Landauer, 2004) (https://www.jstor.org/stable/4166134?seq=1#page_scan_tab_contents).

When Are Goals Most Effective?

Even when goals are SMART, they are not as equally effective. Occasionally, goal setting produces more dramatic effects as compared to all the other methods. Nonetheless, the three conditions that contribute to efficiency have been identified (Latham, 2004; Latham & Locke, 2006) .

Feedback

To work more effectively, workers should receive clear feedback on the progress they are making towards accomplishing their goals. Providing your workers with quantitative figures regarding their sales, defects, or other metrics is extremely useful for feedback purposes. Also, simply telling an employee "job well done" can foster job satisfaction and productivity.

Ability

Employees should have all the skills, knowledge, and abilities which are necessary to reach their goals. In fact, when employees lack the essential abilities, setting specific outcome goals has been shown to lead to lower levels of performance (Seijts & Latham, 2005). People are more likely to feel completely helpless when they lack the skills to reach a goal. Moreover, having specific outcome goals holds them back from focusing completely on learning activities. In such situations, setting goals about learning might be a much better idea. For instance, instead of setting a goal related to increasing sales, the goal could be to identify three methods of getting better acquainted with your clients.

Goal Commitment

SMART goals are more likely to be effective if employees are committed to the goal (Donovan & Radosevich, 1998; Klein et al., 1999; Wofford, Goodwin, & Premack, 1993) (http://psycnet.apa.org/record/1998-01190-014). As a testament to the significance of goal commitment, Microsoft actually calls worker goals "commitments" (Shaw, 2004) (https://dl.acm.org/citation.cfm?id=982403). Goal commitment refers to the degree to which a person is dedicated to reaching the goal.

What makes people dedicated or committed to a goal? Research demonstrates that making goals public might increase commitment to the goal, as it creates accountability to peers. When individuals have a compassionate and trust-based relationship with managers and colleagues, commitment towards goals tend to be higher. When employees participate in goal setting, goal commitment may be higher. Last but not least, rewarding people for their goal accomplishment might also increases commitment to future goals (Klein & Kim, 1998; Latham, 2004; Pritchard et al., 1988) (https://iims.uthscsa.edu/sites/iims/files/Relationships-6.pdf)

Chapter 3: Entrepreneurial Motivation

> *"There is no passion to be found playing small – in settling for a life that is less than the one you are capable of living."* Nelson Mandela (Former South African president)

Are you thinking about starting a small business? Great! But keep in mind that daydreaming and effective planning are two extremely different things. If the focus of your entrepreneurial dreams is centered on the millions of dollars you are going to make, you might need to take a step back and consider your motivations when choosing the kind of small business that you want to start.

The reality is that most small businesses do not make hundreds or thousands of dollars within their first year of operations, or even in their first five years of business. Of course, this *is* possible if you aim high. Regardless, without complete and proper planning, financial backing, and a genuine passion about the products and services you are going to provide to your clients, you will need to take a step back and re-evaluate.

What is Your Passion?

Think about what you like to do and what you are good at doing, not just the possible income. What do you hope to gain from the business in addition to income? If the answer is "nothing," then you might need to reconsider your stance as an entrepreneur, no matter how good your small business idea is. Starting, growing, and running a small business can be an exhausting process, but it can also be extremely gratifying in numerous ways even if you do not make it overnight. So, when the money is not pouring in, will you get disheartened or keep pressing forward? If you are passionate about more than just making money, you will be willing to continue making all the necessary sacrifices until the big bucks to start rolling in.

Many people quit their jobs because they do not like what they are doing and go on to more rewarding jobs. If you start a small business doing something you are not enthusiastic about, do you think there will be any difference between answering clients' emails at 2 a.m. in your pajamas and working for an irritating corporate boss during the day?

Is There a Correlation Between Having the Right Motivation and Starting a Business?

Prosperous entrepreneurs are rarely motivated exclusively by money. Successful business people achieve wealth because they believe in what they are doing and inject their core values into how they build their business. Wealth is their reward, not their goal.

Having a true sense of pride and belief in your own business and products will reflect in everything you do. Your passion and confidence will get other people, clients, and investors excited about your business, and you will have an easier time establishing your small business' credibility.

If your only goal is to make as much money off other people as fast as you can, sooner or later you will make business decisions for the wrong reasons, and eventually hurt your reputation and growth potential. Your integrity will be questioned by your stakeholders.

If your motivation is to start a small business doing something you are extremely ardent about with the goal of making a fulltime living, chances of you suffering emotional setbacks and entrepreneur fatigue are reduced as you focus on building autonomous wealth. You will be more patient with yourself and your business as it grows and will make better business decisions.

Business owners who are wholly and solely motivated by money often have unreasonable expectations of getting rich quick. When monetary goals are your only significant goals, you will miss out on the many other rewards of being self-employed including a sense of accomplishment, purpose, flexibility, and the rewards of knowing you are doing something worthwhile.

What is Entrepreneurial Motivation?

Entrepreneurial motivation is a necessary component that transforms and distinguishes an ordinary individual from an influential businessman who can create opportunities and help in capitalizing on wealth along with economic development. Entrepreneurial motivation is defined as numerous factors which stimulate aspiration and activate enthusiasm in entrepreneurs which make them attain the goals they have set for themselves. Entrepreneurship is the process of recognizing strengths and opportunities which help in the achievement of one's dreams of designing, developing, and running a new business by facing challenges and risks efficiently.

To become an entrepreneur, one should identify his/her opportunities from the external environment. Here, motivation plays a major role in identifying one's own strengths to become strong leaders and powerful entrepreneurs who accept risks and face uncertainty for the purpose of reaching predetermined goals.

Motivation drives entrepreneurs by satisfying higher-level needs such as recognition, esteem, and self-actualization. Various theories have explained motivation as an influencing concept that can bring out hidden talents and creativity and contribute to the individual's goals and social development. Maslow's Hierarchy of Needs theory (http://www.netmba.com/mgmt/ob/motivation/maslow/), Hertzberg's Two-Factor theory (http://www.netmba.com/mgmt/ob/motivation/herzberg/), and David McClelland's Acquired Needs theory (http://www.netmba.com/mgmt/ob/motivation/mcclelland/) prove that motivation can bring energy, enthusiasm, creativity, and efficiency in fulfilling the desired objectives.

Motivation activates innate strengths to achieve a goal. Many questions arise during familiarization with this concept, such as why all human beings can't become leaders or entrepreneurs even though they are exposed to the same motivation. Who can become an effective motivator? What type of motivation can influence one's behavior? Does the extent of motivation decide the power of externalized behavior? Entrepreneurial motivation is a psychological process in which all the motives may not influence the same intensity as it varies with the perception levels of the individuals and the factors responsible for the motivation.

What Is Employee Motivation?

Your employees are your most prized assets and managing them is critical to your business, albeit challenging. This is particularly true for small businesses where employee efficiency is a serious concern. Nevertheless, you cannot blame the workers alone for lower productivity. Employers perform an important function in motivating their employees to become more productive at work. After all, employee satisfaction plays a significant role in boosting productivity and can impact the business' bottom line.

Often, small business owners think that they lack the money or other resources which are required to meet their workers' needs. However, this is far from being true. Most employee motivation approaches require little to no financial investment. It is a simple matter of management adjusting their practices. There are also strategies that do need financial investment, which are usually returned by enhancing employee productivity.

What Makes Employee Motivation Challenging?

Small business owners often face an enormous challenge when it comes to keeping their employees motivated, particularly in environments that fail to make worker satisfaction a part of their fundamental business strategy. While these businesses recognize that they draw their success from the best their workers have to offer, they feel additional

data is needed when it comes to developing motivated and contributing employees. Several issues can lead to demotivating your employees and affect his/her productivity.

Employee's Low Self-Confidence

Confidence enhances workers' level of motivation. It contributes to a
staff member's willingness to continue to complete tasks with utmost
dedication. However, a lack of self-assurance can make a person feel
worthless and unable to make decisions and remain invigorated at
work. It even stops an employee from forming good work relation-
ships. Such workers also tend to procrastinate.

Employee's Lack of Interest in the Work

An interested worker is more likely to act, be curious about a given
task, and work harder to perform it well. A worker who lacks an interest in the business or product, conversely, is less likely to fully engage
in the work and generally perform poorly. Such employees are difficult
to motivate.

Employer's Low Expectations for Success

Positive expectations from personnel act as a motivation factor. The
employer's high expectations often inspire an employee to perform
better. This even increases their self-esteem and makes them more willing to accept challenging assignments in the future. Low expectations,
in contrast, makes workers feel unmotivated and they eventually tend
to underperform. Besides, employers who have little to no expectations from their employees are less likely to capitalize on tools and resources which are necessary to accomplish a given task. This further
reduces the employee's motivation.

Fear of Failure

No one likes to fail. As such, a worker who fears failure tends to avoid
work in which he/she lacks confidence. Such employees mostly per-
ceive a lack of success as failure and shun tasks rather than experienc-
ing shame because of their inability to achieve a goal. The more they
fear failure, the less motivated they are expected to be.

Achievement Anxiety

People who experience low self-esteem are sensitive to reprimands. Mere criticism tends to demotivate them. Achievement anxiety inhibits employee behavior, and such workers are less interested in completing a given task to achieve organizational goals. They often begin a task and stop prior to completion if they become anxious about potential negative feedback.

A lot of these factors are directly related to the office environment, work conditions, and work culture. Managers tend to recruit the best available talent to achieve organizational goals and success without realizing that it is also important to look beneath the surface and consider the workplace environment. It is consequently imperative for employers to implement certain changes in their core strategies in order to boost employee productivity.

Motivational Methods

There are several specific actions that can help increase employee motivation. Even though some of the motivation strategies are specific to either the industry or demographics, some are universal methods every organization needs to follow to improve employee motivation. The best motivation efforts focus on factors that are important to workers.

Different employees have different motivators. It is thus important for organizations to have flexibility within the work scope and reward systems that are designed to improve employee morale and enhance productivity.

The following are some employee motivation methods small businesses can implement without investing a lot of money or resources:

Employee Empowerment

One of the best means to motivate your workers is to give them more responsibility and decision-making power so that they have some control over a given task. This simple strategy goes a long way to reduce frustrations arising from being held accountable for something which they have no control over (for example, lacking enough resources to carry out a task). Moreover, delegating tasks helps free up time for other ad-hoc duties that business owners need to deal with daily.

There is a reason why multi-national companies invest in employee training and professional development programs. It is one of the most beneficial employee retention policies that help you to motivate your people to achieve more by enhancing their skills. All you need to do is provide the required tools and opportunities for your workers to accomplish more. Chances are most of your staff will take on this challenge and your business will benefit.

Accreditation and licensing programs are effective in improving employee knowledge and motivation and are in great demand. Management education and interactions with thought leaders also provide a deeper understanding of business to your employees and can improve their attitudes toward the company and clients, while boosting self-confidence.

However, providing training and professional development opportunities is not enough. You must make sure that employees are able to apply the knowledge gained to complete their work and further enhance their contributions to your company. In other words, the acquisition of knowledge and skills must be worthwhile for both the employee and employer to influence motivation; otherwise, it is just a waste of time, money and effort.

Encourage Innovation and Creativity

Businesses where employees hesitate to express their original ideas to management for fear of being ignored or mocked may miss out on some groundbreaking concepts to increase employee morale. In fact, both the worker and the business suffer from such practices.

A better approach is to empower personnel to make decisions within the confines of their duties while limiting unnecessary administrative red tape. Give opportunities for workers who know the jobs or products/services best to use their ideas for further development. Encourage the exchange of intuitive information and ideas among your employees and departments. This way you are using your employees' experience more wisely and making them feel valued and appreciated.

These strategies will not only improve employee morale within the organization, but also help in producing a more flexible working environment as it creates an openness to change. Furthermore, you will be positioned to react quickly to market changes as well as gain first-mover advantages in the marketplace.

Financial Incentives

According to the SHRM 2014 survey, (https://www.shrm.org/hr-to-day/trends-and-forecasting/research-and-surveys/Documents/2016-Employee-Job-Satisfaction-and-Engagement-Report.pdf) compensation tops the list of aspects that contribute to employee job satisfaction. Money is one of the most important factors in motivating employees to become more productive. It is, therefore, no surprise that many businesses share their profits with employees in the form of incentives.

Financial incentives motivate personnel to produce quality products, offer quality service, and/or improve the overall quality of the organizational process. It is important to make your workforce realize that what benefits the company also benefits them directly. You can provide monetary incentives for various purposes such as:

1. Generating process-improving and cost-saving ideas;

2. Reducing absenteeism; and

3. Enhancing productivity.

On the downside, the motivating effects of money (even though effective) are short-lived. In addition, it must be made accessible to employees based on their contributions to the company's success. You should thus couple monetary incentives with nonmonetary motivators.

WHAT ARE SMALL WINS?

When a company wins a major client, signs a great contract or successfully finishes a big project, it is the time for celebrations. However, what happens to those smaller victories, the ones that often make the backbone of a company's success? Are they celebrated too, or are they just omitted and taken for granted? If you aren't celebrating small wins, you might be missing some great opportunities to become an even better leader and motivate your team. In fact, the most successful and popular bosses tend to celebrate every victory, no matter the size. Here's why you should consider doing the same if you want to get the best out of your team.

1. To remember your overall goal

2. To emphasize goal-setting

3. To boost motivation

4. To show your company's success

5. To break up the work

6. To reward specifics

Nonmonetary Incentives

Studies (http://www.academia.edu/) indicate that non-monetary incentives are operational tools, which can be used for motivating employees. As previously mentioned, there are certain downsides of using monetary systems as motivators. Expectations in such cases often exceed results; whereby disparity in salaries among individuals can cause division instead of unity in the workforce.

Nonmonetary incentives that serve as positive motivators(http://www.vitaver.com/blog/2010/07 /6-non-monetary-rewards-that-motivate- employees/) include responsibility, recognition, and advancement. Employers and managers also need to recognize employees' small wins (https://hbr.org/2011/05/the- power-of-small-wins) to promote participatory environments. In addition, it is imperative to treat all employees equally with fairness and respect to create highly motivated workers.

Other effective non-monetary rewards include time off from work, letters of commendation, enhanced personal fulfillment, and sincere praise from peers and the upper management. Such personal gestures are among the most effective employee motivators. When combined with monetary rewards, these programs have the potential to satisfy the intrinsic and self-actualizing needs of your workforce.

Quality of Life

The United States is the world's most overworked developed nation. In fact, the number of working hours each week is increasing for American workers. Reports suggest that full-time workers in the U.S. are working 47 hours on average weekly. As a result, many workers don't have a quality life beyond the workplace. This has an adverse effect on an employee's morale and productivity.

Companies with flexible employment arrangements can easily reduce such negatives and motivate employees for increased productivity. Many are incorporating programs like flextime, job sharing, and condensed workweeks to help employees meet the demands of their personal lives and at the same time accomplish the given tasks at work successfully.

Chapter 4: Legal and Business Structures

"Chase the vision, not the money; the money will end up following you."
Tony Hsieh (CEO Of Zappos)

One of the countless roles you will have to play in your small business is like that of a security guard. You must ensure that your business remains safe and that nothing harmful to your business enters. Conversely, be on the lookout for anything leaving your business that could diminish its value. The more you can use legal protections to shield your business, the easier this task becomes.

There are several different means to protect your business, its assets, and employees. One such way is to conduct business within the most appropriate legal framework. The framework used to support your small business can influence your tax payments, liability, and potential for future investment.

As an entrepreneur, you must make decisions and take legal actions to structure your business. Failure to do so can lead to consequences that can be very detrimental. Even if you have never formally selected a legal structure for your business, you are nonetheless operating within such parameters. States usually consider unregistered businesses as being sole proprietorships or partnerships, leaving you personally responsible for liabilities.

What Factors Determine the Best Business Structure?

While it is essential to consider several factors when determining the legal structure of your business, not all aspects are going to apply to each company. Several important issues, however, apply to most entities.

Control

Who is the primary decision maker? The decision maker has the power to control management, determine who receives profits, and decide whether to get loans or solicit investors. This individual is exclusively responsible for the business's financial losses.

Taxes

Tax liability is a significant concern for small business owners. The amount of taxes paid annually can make or break a business.

Liability

Some legal structures do not protect personal assets from business debts. If you do not want to be personally liable for the debts of your small business, consider a legal structure that will protect your individual assets.

Transferability of Ownership

The legal structure elected can determine the transferability of a person's ownership to another in whole or in part simply by the exchange of a piece of paper.

Longevity of the Business

Not all small business structures are long-lasting. Some forms of organization cease when the entrepreneur relinquishes operations.

Raising Capital

Simple entities, for example, sole proprietorships and general partnerships are restricted in their capacity to raise capital.

Most often, entrepreneurs are concerned with all these significant issues. The key is to identify the legal structure that best meets your individual and business requirements while accommodating organizational growth. This tough but crucial decision should be made with adequate counsel from an attorney, accountant, or other advisers.

Most Common Legal Structures to Consider

It is imperative to take time to thoroughly understand the different ways to establish your business while factoring in personal circumstances, the size of your business, and your plans for growth

Sole Proprietorship

A sole proprietorship is a business with one owner and is the most common form of business organization in the U.S. and includes over 23 million people according to a 2014 survey of US businesses. (https://taxfoundation.org/us-has-more-individually-owned-businesses-corporations). This type of business represents 73% of all businesses in the U.S. today.

A sole proprietor business is the most natural business type to start and operate. Unlike corporations and LLCs, you do not have to formally register your business with the state. Some disadvantages exist with a sole proprietor business, as follows:

Advantages of Sole Proprietorship

1. Owners have the power to establish sole proprietorship instantly, easily, and without incurring high costs.

2. The owner is not liable to pay unemployment tax on himself/herself.

3. Sole proprietorships carry little to no ongoing formalities, if any.

4. The owner maintains 100% control of the business, thus making decisions relatively easy.

5. No separate tax return is required. Income or loss flows through to the owner's personal return.

Disadvantages of Sole Proprietorship

1. Sole proprietorships seldom survive the incapacity of the owners and so do not maintain value.

2. The unlimited personal obligation binds the owner for the debts, losses, and liabilities of the business.

3. Owners will not be able to raise capital by selling an interest in the business.

4. The owner is liable for self-employment tax on ordinary business income (generally 15.3%).

Limited Liability Company

Many states in the U.S. allow a business form called the limited liability company (LLC). The LLC arose from business owners' desire to adopt a business structure permitting them to limit their liability exposure. If structured as a partnership, the operating agreement outlines the partners' roles, income, and loss distribution, and the aftermath in the event of a partner's demise. In general, unless the business owner establishes a separate corporation, the owner and partners (if any) assume complete liability for all debts of the business. Under the LLC rules, however, an individual is not responsible for the firm's debt, provided he or she didn't secure it personally by obtaining a second mortgage, a personal line of credit, or by risking personal assets.

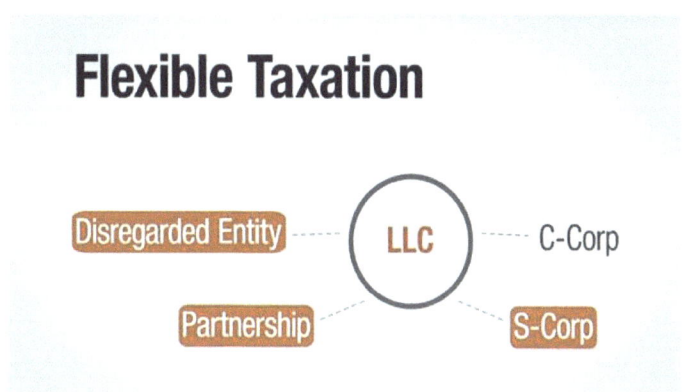

Advantages of an LLC

1. Pass-through taxation.

2. No limitations on the number of members allowed.

3. Members have flexibility in structuring the organization's management.

4. Requires less administrative filing and paperwork than corporations.

5. Members are not individually responsible for business debts and other liabilities.

6. Provides flexibility in taxation since the entity can elect to be taxed as a sole proprietorship, partnership, S Corporation, or C Corporation.

7. Provides protection for real estate investors because each LLC can be designed to acquire its own properties.

Disadvantages of an LLC

1. Comparatively more expensive than sole proprietorships and general partnerships.

2. Ownership is usually more difficult to transfer.

3. No uniformity because of variation in treatment by different states.

4. Members are subject to self-employment tax if S Corp election is not made.

Partnership
A partnership involves two or more people going into business together intending to make a profit. There are two types of partnerships: general and limited.

1. A **general partnership** is created informally, and partners are agents of the partnership. There is no need to file documents with the state before starting. The formation can be either written, oral, or implied.

2. A **limited partnership** has at least one general partner who controls the company's day-to-day operations and is personally liable for business debts, and passive partners called limited partners. This form of partnership requires government approval with a charter including the names of all general partners. The limited partner neither has the right to use partnership property, nor input in the daily management of the business.

A limited partner contributes a defined amount of capital to the business, but is generally not liable for its debts or obligations.

Advantages of Partnerships

1. Two heads are better than one. This can lead to better work/life balance and sharing of ideas.

2. It is relatively straightforward to change the legal structure down the road.

3. Relatively low start-up costs.

4. Limited external protocols.

5. More capital available for business purposes.

6. Income or loss is passed through to the partners for tax purposes.

Disadvantages of Partnerships

1. Liabilities of the business are unlimited.

2. There is a chance of disagreement and friction between the partners.

3. Loss of autonomy and control over business decisions.

4. A separate tax return must be filed by the partnership, thus increasing the administrative burden.

Limited Liability Partnership

Limited liability partnerships (LLPs) is a form of partnership for professionals such as doctors, lawyers, accountants and engineers. They help limit the owners' personal liability for business debts while enjoying some of the benefits of pass-through taxation.

Advantages of Limited Liability Partnership

1. Offers liability protection.

2. Partners are held responsible only for any acts of negligence they commit.

3. Taxes flow through to the partners' individual tax returns.

Disadvantages of Limited Liability Partnership

1. Some states do not recognize LLPs as legal business structures.

2. Considered non-partnerships by certain taxing authorities in some states.

Corporation

A corporate structure used to be the most common way to start a business because the corporation exists as a separate entity. This is usually referred to as a C Corporation. In general, a corporation has all the legal rights of an individual, except for the right to vote and certain other limitations. Corporations are given the right to exist by the state that issues their charter. If you incorporate in one state to take advantage of liberal corporate laws but do business in another state, you'll have to file for "qualification" in the state in which you wish to operate the business. There is usually a fee to qualify to conduct business in a state.

Advantages of Corporation

1. Limited liability to the shareholders.

2. Easy transfer of ownership.

3. Perpetual life since the death of the owners does not lead to a termination of the business.

Disadvantages of Corporation

1. Double taxation as income is taxed at the corporate and individual level.

2. Independent management by the board of directors and not the shareholders.

3. Excessive tax filings through different types of taxes and paperwork administration.

S Corporation

The S corporation is often more attractive to small business owners than a standard corporation generally known as a C Corporation. The underlying reason is that an S corporation has some appealing tax benefits and still provides business owners with the liability protection of a corporation. With an S corporation, income and losses are passed through to shareholders and included on their individual tax returns. As a result, there's just one level of federal tax.

Certain conditions need to exist to be eligible for a subchapter S election.

- The corporation cannot have more than 100 shareholders (husband and wife count as one shareholder unless they divorce).

- The following entities may be shareholders: individuals, estates, and certain trusts.

- Shareholders must be either citizens or residents of the United States.

- There can only be one class of stock.

- It must be a domestic corporation.

Advantages of S Corporation

1. Protected assets through limited liability.

2. Pass-through taxation.

3. Tax-favorable characterization of income.

4. Straightforward transfer of ownership.

Disadvantages of S Corporation

1. Taxable fringe benefits.

2. Formation and ongoing expenses.

3. Less flexibility in allocating income and loss.

4. Tax qualification obligations.

5. Potential closer IRS scrutiny.

6. Stock ownership restrictions.

Carefully choosing your business structure can have long range consequences from a tax and liability perspective. It is commonly miscon-
strued that organizing an LLC with the secretary of state generates potential tax savings. The main purpose of setting up an LLC is for asset
protection purposes. An LLC can elect to be taxed a single member
(Schedule C), partnership (Form 1065), S Corp (Form 1120s), and C
Corp (Form 1120). LLCs are ideal for passive income (rentals interest
and dividends from stocks and bonds) because of the avoidance of
self-employment tax. Most experts recommend electing an S Corp sta-
tus for operational businesses. Chapter 9 of this book elaborates more
on the various tax implications that a small business may encounter.

Chapter 5: Professional Teams

"My model for business is The Beatles. They were four guys who kept each other's kind of negative tendencies in check. They balanced each other, and the total was greater than the sum of the parts. That's how I see business: great things in business are never done by one person, they're done by a team of people ". Steve Jobs (Visionary and Founder of Apple)

You know your clients. You have a fantastic product to sell. You prepared the business plan. Your strategies are well documented, and all the funds are in place. You are ready to go to market and even prepared for explosive growth. However, are you sure you are surrounded by the best possible teammates to make your dream a reality?

Most new entrepreneurs prefer to work alone when they are developing their ideas or solutions to a problem. However, they ultimately realize that starting and growing a business requires so much more.

Not many people have the expertise to cover all the necessary bases concurrently. These areas include finance, marketing, manufacturing, and operations along with solution development. It takes a collaborative team to build any small business.

What many budding entrepreneurs don't realize is that building a team is just as critical and challenging as building business solutions. If you recruit the wrong people in your group, or the team you assemble cannot work together, you limit chances of building a successful business no matter how great your productis.

According to a Forbes article (https://www.forbes.com/sites/danschaw-bel/2017/11/01/10-workplace-trends-youll-see-in-2018/#61bf22664bf2), 60% of small business owners and bosses state their biggest human resources challenge is hiring skilled talent. Heavy competition for employees with specialized skills doubles the struggle of budget crunches imposed on recruiters. Some small businesses with deep pockets offer generous transition packages to lure workers away from their competitors. For the small businesses that cannot afford this, smarter team building strategies arerequired.

How to Build a Strong Team

Identify your Needs

Start by knowing your future business goals. A thorough review of your organizational chart, functions, and employees will help you pin-point the gaps between your current talent and missing skills. You should consider both the short-term openings and the long-term needs. This will factor in how your business expansion, employee changes, and industry development may affect your personnel require-ments.

Once you identify all the areas which require you to recruit people, you can begin considering your hiring options. Do you need full-time staff members, part-time employees, ongoing vendors, or project contrac-tors? Once you have successfully identified the required positions, you need to develop the right recruiting strategy.

Write a profile for your ideal candidate, describing their skill set, level of experience, and desirable work habits. Build this into a job descrip-tion which provides value to the prospective recruits in exchange for the skills you are seeking. What can you offer to talented employees to make them want to work for you instead of your competitors?

Hire Based on Culture as well as Qualifications

The person who has all the right qualifications isn't necessarily the best choice for your small business. The most essential aspect of your business is your culture. Consistently look for team members who inspire, maintain, and build your business's current culture. When your environment is fast-paced and upbeat, it won't help to hire people who are slow to act and lack suitable social skills.

When you build a team that gets along, they will be happier, and happier teams always do better work. While you are doing culture fit screenings, ask open-ended questions which reveal something about a candidate's personality. One of the best questions to ask during these interviews is "Tell me a story." It can also be helpful to present an applicant with a "real work" scenario to evaluate how he/she would handle the situation. These questions force people to think on their feet, and you learn about their personal style. You could also use formal personality tests to screen new hires.

Engage and Motivate

The real work begins after you have hired the best possible people for your organization. There are a lot of small business owners who assign large, important projects to new employees and hope for the best. It is easy to understand why they do this. Entrepreneurs want things done yesterday. So, you hire team members and delegate work that you don't have time due to preoccupation with other pressing needs.

However, if you don't make an effort to show your employees that you notice and appreciate the work they are doing, there is a considerable risk that they will lose interest and motivation. Most employees are looking for constructive feedback, even if it is negative. What matters is that this feedback comes from somebody they believe is trying to help them improve. Sincere praise for a job well done will go a long way towards building a strong bond of trust.

Set Clear Expectations

If you hire the correct people, they will be smart and hardworking. They would want to succeed. Most of all they would want to feel that they are contributing to something bigger than themselves. It is your job as a boss to lay out a convincing vision and crystal-clear expectations. You should present new hires with a job description and /or a written policy manual. They can also work with a mentor during the probationary phase as the get acclimated to the company's operations.

Ensure that every person on your team has individual goals and knows how those goals relate to your business' overall objectives. Give them clear guidelines and all the resources they need. Communicate small victories and policy changes to all employees so that they feel they are an essential part of the team, and thus remain committed to its success.

Every Successful Team Has Key Players

The Leader
The success of any business starts with the leader. The best business coaches are "servant leaders," someone who shares power. They recognize that their business will soar if they hire amazing people and let them own their assignments. The team leader is there to support the efforts the employees are putting in, with the required resources, and guiding principles. The leader will encourage, motivate, reward, and provide feedback on their job performance. Your team leader is going to correct your workers with kindness and will also celebrate their achievements. If you choose the right leader, he/she will be a role model for the employees.

The Expert
Small businesses succeed because they hire people who know the industry, trends, competitors, market, clients, products, vendors, and investors. Utilizing an expert will help you generate more return on investment (ROI). They will surround themselves with workers, managers, and other leaders who are most likely to benefit your organization.

Experts bring valuable information, along with in-depth knowledge of their assignments. They also will be willing to share what they know with all the other team members. These specialists will mentor others who are learning the business. They are vigilant and therefore, continue to learn. They also provide guidance and wisdom on what works and does not work in the organization, which results in fewer mistakes and a higher level of productivity.

The Financial Guru

Successful small businesses have a skilled and experienced financial officer. Do not minimize the importance of this critical leader. No organization can prosper without someone who understands accounting, finance, strategy, and cash flow management. There should be someone on the team who can be trusted with funds that are received and disbursed by the company. Often, this individual has the title of treasurer. Whoever owns this position should know about the financial health of the company, as well as the cash flow at any time. It is also worth mentioning that proper financial planning not only helps improve your bottom line, but also reduces the amount of taxes you pay.

The Strategist

Having a strategist on your team is another important role which helps your organization prosper. Most entrepreneurs approach their business from a big picture perspective as they juggle multiple demands. They are concentrating on ensuring that the business makes money.

Strategists have knowledge about the emerging trends in the industry, changes in consumer behavior, their competitors, and disruptive product innovations. Therefore, having a such an expert to take care of these crucial elements is very important for any team.

The Doer

Every great business has someone who owns the responsibility to do what's necessary to execute the company plans. These assignments might encompass research, human resources, inventory management, marketing, manufacturing, and sales. In several organizations, the person who oversees all these tasks bears the title of chief operating officer.

The successful requirement for carrying out each of the above roles and responsibilities entails the hiring of an expert staff of team members with specific duties. These employees are the heart of the business and deliver what the clients want and buy. Organizations that typically nosedive do not have these key people on their team.

Chapter 6: Accounting Software

"Don't ever let your business get ahead of the financial side of your business. Accounting, accounting, accounting. Know your numbers". Tilman J. Fertita (American Billionaire and TV Personality)

Accounting systems should be used to prepare the organization's operating budget and track the expenditures and income. Accounting systems can also handle payroll, taxes, and various other business transactions such as workers' compensation, healthcare coverage, and other benefits.

Functions of business accounting can be handled in-house or outsourced to an accounting firm. Failure to correctly manage your accounting system may result in financial disaster.

How to Avoid Accounting Errors

Even though it can be helpful to process all transactions quickly and without a hassle by using high powered accounting software, hiring someone to correct mistakes down the line is something you want to avoid. Understanding various kinds of accounting mistakes businesses commonly make can be the difference between having to pay to fix an error and getting it correct the first time.

The following are some accounting mistakes which some small business owners make, and how to steer clear of them.

Accidentally Recording Transactions in a Prior Period

Once you have closed your accounting books for the accounting period (monthly, quarterly or annually), you really should not go back to change them, unless recommended by an accounting professional. Such corrections usually come with amending tax returns for the year in question. Some accounting applications might not allow you to close the prior period's financial statements. This can lead to posting current year transactions in the prior period. This could have an adverse effect because your financial statements might not match what's on last the year's tax returns and could lead to serious issues if you are ever audited for tax purposes.

Incorrect Asset or Liability Balances

Asset accounts must have debit balances, and liability accounts must have credit balances. One of the most common causes of an improper balance in these balance sheet accounts is posting entries to the improper general ledger account, misclassifying accounts, and repeatedly adjusting entries.

Incorrect Revenue or Expense Entries

Revenue accounts should have credit balances, and expense accounts should have debit balances. Issues generally result from posting entries to the incorrect account, misclassifying accounts, and duplicating adjusting entries, which are the same reasons for having incorrect balances in balance sheet accounts.

Misclassifying Expenses

Small business accounting systems save time as entries are entered and posted very quickly and effortlessly. However, when accounting information is entered, an operator can easily pick the wrong general ledger account and/or expense description. Misclassifying expenses not only results in incorrect accounting, but also can lead to financial reporting and tax preparation red flags.

Delegate When Needed

You might have heard the expression "penny wise and pound foolish" about people who spend hours of their time to save a few dollars. You have to realize that your job is to run your business. A worker builds, a painter paints, and a realtor sells. It is important to delegate work to a finance specialist within your organization. It is equally important to seek outside help from a professional such as an attorney or accountant, when needed.

Functions of Accounting Software

According to a Forbes magazine article (https://www.forbes.com/sites/bernardmarr/2018/06/01/the-digital-transformation-of-accounting-and-finance-artificial-intelligence-robots-and-chatbots/#606ea2d94ad8), artificial intelligence will continue to play a tremendous role in accounting and finance. Business applications will be more than just number crunchers and will be valuable in providing data analytics to business executives with minimal human errors. It a common misconception that only finance and accounting professionals need accounting software. A good commercial accounting software not only helps with bookkeeping tasks, but also provides reports and forecasting to track sources and uses of funds (https://financesonline.com/accounting-software-analysis-features-types-benefits-pricing/).

If you do choose to use accounting software, be sure to choose wisely. Some of the important features to look for in software includes:

- Accounting: The primary function of this software entails recording and reporting transactions to help generate profit and loss, balance sheets, and cash flow reports. This simplified process handles double-entry accounting behind the scenes thus alleviating clerical staff from making complicated journal entries requiring debits and credits. These transactions reside in the general ledger (GL) under the fixed assets, accounts receivable, accounts payable, inventory modules, etc.

- Payroll Management: This software helps set up, calculate, and process employee payments while ensuring that federal and state taxes are appropriately withheld.

- Billing and Invoicing: A basic accounting software will help users process invoices their customers (cash in-flows). It helps identify who owes the company, the balance, and the ageing of an account to facilitate proper and timely collections. Some software even offers the capability to automatically invoice and receive payments on a periodic basis.

- Inventory Management: For businesses with inventory, proper managing of SKUs and stock count is a requirement. Accounting software can help monitor and track location, determine costing, and send alerts when minimum levels are reached.

- Fixed Asset Management: Not all purchases are to be expensed and deducted in a reporting period according to Generally Accepted Accounting Principles (GAAP) and IRS rules. Through proper fixed asset management, an organization can record major purchases and depreciate these expenditures over the asset's useful life.

Benefits of Accounting Software

Budget Planning

Small businesses should plan their budget to ensure their operation stays on the right track. The budget process includes assessing the financial needs of a business and generating a financial roadmap to ensure vendors and employees are paid timely, while staying on course with earnings as well as income projections. Businesses which fail to use a proper accounting system face the risk of underestimating expenses or overestimating earnings, both of which can eventually lead to business failure.

Accounts Payable

Accounts payable are those bills a business pays when covering its various operating costs. Without an appropriate accounting system, accounts might be paid late or not at all, which can result in a range of different problems. A company can see product delivery stop, utilities turned off, insurance coverage dropped, or other disastrous consequences. Any one of these problems can impact a business's productivity and viability.

Accounts Receivable

Knowing the origin (sources) of your revenue is equally as important as knowing its destination (uses). A proper accounting system tracks sales and income and guarantees that clients are paying as expected. A business that allows unpaid accounts to go uncollected and provides services or delivers products without compensation puts itself at huge financial risk. For a small business with very low profit margins, losing money in this manner can lead to a significant financial deficit, which could potentially result in bankruptcy.

Tax Preparation

A small business in-house accounting expert can handle tax groundwork for the business or can work alongside an outside tax accounting firm. Regardless of how a business handles this preparation, proper accounting procedures implemented throughout the year can help guarantee that all tax obligations are being fulfilled. The organization accomplishes this through detailed financial record-keeping. A business that fails to handle tax payments and filings timely and appropriately runs the risk of tax penalties and fines that can become substantial and cause damage to a business' operation.

Embezzling

Lack of a proper accounting system can lead to a company's funds being misappropriated due to lack of internal controls. Internal controls help monitor and direct a firm's resources. A dishonest employee could take advantage of lax accounting procedures to slowly but steadily siphon money from your company, thus resulting in financial insolvency and business failure. Understanding how to develop and read balance sheets, profit and loss statements (P&L), and cash flow reports will help better manage and protect your business.

Chapter 7: Capital and Budgeting

"You can have everything in life you want, if you will just help other people get what they want." Zig Ziglar (American Author, Salesman and Motivational Speaker)

There is an expression which states, "People don't plan to fail, they just fail to plan." No entrepreneur who plans to go into business fails on purpose. Access (or lack thereof) to working capital along with other financial options is a significant contributor to any business' lack of success or ultimate failure.

There are several different factors which go into an entrepreneur's lack of working capital, ranging from a low credit score and inability to borrow from traditional financing sources to operational issues which affect the cash flow.

A business owner needs to understand the root cause of their financial problems. This knowledge will help you work with financiers, thus ensuring that the business stays afloat.

How Does the Lack of Funding Hurt Your Business?

Your business depends heavily on its ability to sell products or services, get paid timely, meet financial obligations, replenish inventory (if applicable) to expand and grow. Within this chain are numerous factors which independently threaten your ability to meet future responsibilities and may lead to business failure. To ensure sustainability and build up working capital, current assets should always exceed current liabilities.

One of the components that affects your current assets is your accounts receivable. When you work with clients who are slow players or are out of cycle with your accounts payable or bills you pay, you wind up with a cash flow situation which is untenable over time. Having enough cash reserves available to you to close those gaps during downtimes would be ideal for most small businesses. However, your business ultimately suffers when you cannot access funding sources like the ones traditionally offered by banks and other conventional financial institutions.

Cash Flow Mistakes to Avoid

No matter how amazing and lucrative your business model is, or how many potential investors are interested in supporting your business, the company will not survive if you are unable to manage your business' cash flow. A famous study from the financial services company U.S. Bank discovered that almost 82 percent of startups and small businesses fail due to poor cash-flow management. (https://www.entrepreneur.com/article/187366). So, even if you are an excellent entrepreneur in every other way, you should stay squarely focused on managing your company's cash flow to avoid putting your business in harm's way.

Engaging in Impulsive Spending During the Startup Phase

"It takes money to make money." We hear this so often in business, and in several ways, it seems valid. Unfortunately, this belief can make many entrepreneurs fall prey to overspending, especially in the first few months of business. The reality is that even though the above adage may sometimes hold true, not all small business expenses are created equal.

Starting any business involves a lot of beneficial expenses, *i.e.* expenses which are going to benefit your company's profitability in quantifiable ways. However, there are also several consultants, advisers, and business-to-business (B2B) service providers who would be very happy to take your startup's capital for things you do not need. If you want your business to make money, it is imperative to keep your eye on the bottom line, considering the cost vs benefit of every expense. After all, every dollar you spend on your small business is a dollar which will ultimately reduce your profit margin.

Along with the revenue forecasts, create a realistic budget and make sure you stick to it. Calculate when you plan for your business to break even, and as unexpected expenses or opportunities for impulsive spending arise, go back to your projections and calculate how all these purchases are going to delay your breakeven point. You might decide that your workers do not need that ping pong table after all.

Accurate Future Sales Estimates

Relentless optimism is one of the essential traits of successful entrepreneurs. What realistic person is going to persevere in the face of so many different obstacles, so many naysayers, and so much stress? However, even though optimism is critical for any new business owner, letting it compromise your objectivity might become dangerous to your cash flow. Remember not every interested customer is going to make a purchase.

Although your sales volume might increase over the holidays, expecting it to double is a little unrealistic. Therefore, it is vital to predict objective and realistic sales using historical evidence as well as real numbers. By applying quantitative forecasting methods, you may use actual past revenue data from your business or even other businesses in your industry as a basis for tracking trends and predicting future sales. This information, along with some business instincts, is going to help you come up with more realistic future sales projections.

Revenue forecasting can become particularly challenging in the first five years of business, as you do not have past sales figures or enough other empirical data to utilize. This is where working with a mentor from within your industry might be very useful. A good business mentor might offer his/her own experience to help you project your future sales. No matter which method you go for, it is crucial that you base future sales expectations on objective facts along with sound judgment. Paying attention to the above concepts is going to keep you within the confines of your budget.

Using a Cash Flow Statement

Let's assume you have set realistic expectations for future sales. You have established spending limits and are doing everything possible to make your customers pay up in a timely manner. These three factors can improve your business' long-term cash flow; however, lack of tracking your day-to-day cash flow can lead to your business still finding itself in a financial impasse.

Retail businesses typically experience financial difficulties the months before the holidays. You require more inventory from your suppliers to prepare for an influx of sales. Nonetheless, if those suppliers' payments are due before your sales happen, you might have trouble paying your bills on time.

Using a cash flow statement is going to help you track your inflow of revenue and outflow of expenses during a specific period. This is going to help you anticipate when you have more money going out than coming in so that you can plan for the trying times ahead. Without any cash flow statement, you are just guessing at whether you will have the money you require when needed, thus increasing your chances of facing late payments and all the other penalties associated with past due invoices.

Be Proactive About Receivables

One of the fastest cash flow killers, particularly for small businesses, results from unpaid customer invoices due to being passive about collecting payments from your customers. Businesses that do not have robust late payment penalties or collections policies in place are often taken advantage of. If your customers do not know for sure that they will hear from you the moment a payment is late, you are going to be the last of their vendors to get paid.

If you have not already done so, set clear policies with your clients for late payment penalties. Good strategies include a 5% late penalty after a certain number of days, and a work stoppage after 30 days past due. Create an internal timeline of the procedures for when you will send the initial invoice, when payment reminders go out, and when you will make collection phone calls or cut off the services if past invoices have not been paid. Some businesses have even benefited from incentivizing clients through discounts for early payments.

Keep a Cushion of Cash on Hand

No matter how many safeguards you have in place to protect your business' cash, setbacks in cash flow are a business reality. This might be no big deal if you have a cushion of savings on hand. However, if your business is working from a zero-account balance, one slow sales month may mean instant disaster. To safeguard your business from cash flow issues, you should maintain an account balance equivalent to at least two months of the operating costs. This way, even if you undergo unexpected stalls to cash flow, you have reserves in place to protect yourself.

Sources of Short-Term and Long-Term Financing for Working Capital

A continuous flow of working capital is an essential component of a successful business. Expenses that must be paid regardless of cash inflow include but are not limited to:

1. Salaries and wages

2. Raw materials and inventory

3. Rent and utility bills

4. Equipment servicing

5. Marketing and advertising

6. Other general overhead costs

Funds are required to cover these expenses until the clients make their payment. Working capital is the lifeblood of any small business. There are two kinds of financing: short-term and long-term.

Short-Term Financing

Banks can be a valuable source when it comes to short-term working capital finance. Several sources of financing an operation's short-range expenses abound.

1. Overdraft Agreement

By entering into an overdraft agreement with the bank, the bank will allow the business to borrow up to a certain limit without the requirement for further discussion. The bank may ask for security in the form of collateral and may charge daily interest at a capricious rate on the outstanding debt. An overdraft agreement is a precious source of financing and one that many small businesses resort to if the business is confident in making the repayments quickly.

2. Accounts Receivable Financing

Many banks and non-banking financial institutions offer invoice discounting services. The company takes the commercial bills to the bank which makes the reimbursement while charging a small fee. On the fixed due date, the bank collects the money from the clients. This is another conventional method of financing utilized by a variety of businesses. Organizations which offer broad terms of credit can carry on their operations without having to wait for the clients to settle their bills.

3. Customer Advances

Numerous companies insist on the client making an advance payment before selling them goods or providing a service. This is very effective when it comes to dealing with huge orders that take a long time to finalize. This method also makes sure that the business has some funds to channel into its operations for fulfilling those orders.

4. Selling Goods on Installment

Many businesses, particularly those that sell electronics, jewelry, refrigerators, vehicles, etc., allow clients to make their payments in installments. Not all customers can afford the cost of the product immediately, but are still real potential buyers. In such cases, instead of waiting for a large payment at the end, some companies allow the customers to make regular monthly payments. An installment plan ensures that there is a constant flow of funds coming into the business that does not prolong the accounts receivable cycle

Long-Term Financing
Relying purely on short-term funds to meet working capital needs is not always practical, especially for industries where the production itself takes a long time such as automobiles, real estate development, aircraft, refrigerators, and computers. Such businesses need their working capital to last for a long time and must think about long-term financing.

1. Long-Term Bank Loans

Many small businesses go for a full-fledged long-term loan from a bank that lets them meet all their working capital requirements for two, three, or more years.

2. Retained Earnings

Rather than making the dividend payments to stakeholders or investing in new ventures, many businesses retain a portion of their profits to use for working capital. This way they do not have to take loans, pay interest, or suffer losses on discounted bills; thus, they can be autonomous in their financing.

Businesses cannot rely only on limited sources for their working capital requirements. They need to tap into various avenues. They also need to continuously evaluate their needs through analysis of financial statements and financial ratios, and thereupon choose their working capital channels carefully. This is an ongoing process, and different routes are suitable at different points in time. The trick is to choose the right alternative based on the individual situation.

Chapter 8: Commingling Business and Personal Funds

> *"Timing, perseverance, and ten years of trying will eventually make you look like an overnight success." Biz Stone (co-founder of Twitter)*

Even though some business owners know how to keep their business assets separate from their personal assets, a preponderance of small business owners fails to adhere to this principle. Combining such funds is not a good idea from a legal, logistical, and tax standpoint. When you pay a lawyer or even a government entity to set up a business structure such as an LLC or a Corporation, it is always a smart idea to separate business and personal transactions to avoid administrative issues.

This is a crucial step needed to keep the limited liability component of your business. In legal terms, there is a business concept known as the 'corporate veil' which is the liability shield between a business entity and an individual. When one commingles business and personal funds, the courts can pierce this corporate veil and get into your personal assets thereby bypassing the liability protection of your company. This mistake also has tax-related implications.

What Is Commingling of Funds?

Just like the phrase sounds, commingling funds involves the mixing of both personal and business funds in one account. Nevertheless, it can include using business funds to pay for personal expenses, and vice versa. There are some business owners who use their organization's bank account as an extension of their individual bank account. Some of the most common ways through which you could commingle funds inadvertently are as follows:

1. Withdrawing money from your company's account in order to pay personal expenses without proper documentation.

2. Transferring money between your business and personal accounts without appropriate documentation.

3. Depositing your business checks in your private bank account.

4. Writing business checks for personal expenses and vice versa.

5. Having a shared account bank account for both personal and business needs.

It is essential to keep your corporate veil intact. Fundamentally, all the effort you put in while forming the LLC such as filing the Articles of Organization, paying the attorney or filing fees, and perhaps drafting the Operating Agreement will be in vain when it comes to limiting liability. Creditors will be able to reach your personal assets once you commingle.

Reasons to Avoid Commingling Funds

One of the basics of operating any small business is setting up a business bank account. This fundamental business function is often ignored by both new and even seasoned business professionals who comingle personal funds with their business funds. Comingling funds is common among moonlighters such as multi-level marketers and self-employed sole proprietors, realtors as well as consultants.

Business owners with a small staff often try to process business transactions using their personal bank accounts to reduce their expenses and bank fees. When you fall into any one of these categories, you might be creating potential problems for your business. The following are some reasons why you should separate your business bank account from your personal bank account.

Tax Problems

When tax season rolls around and you must present the profit and loss statement needed to prepare taxes to your accountant, only business-related transactions will count as deductible expenses. Misclassifications stemming from deliberate or negligent lack of segregation between business and personal transactions can result in your tax return being flagged for an audit, thus risking accuracy-related penalties and interest. Therefore, it is advisable to keep separate accounts for both your business and personal funds.

The Hobby/Business Classification

As stated above, per the Internal Revenue Service (IRS), only business transactions can be written off for tax purposes. There are also specific guidelines to determine whether an entity is a business or a personal hobby. If the expenses incurred while running your company go through the personal bank account, you might be giving the IRS the impression that your business is a hobby. Additionally, the failure to show a profit (usually 3 out of 5 years) may trigger that perception. The IRS would question your business motives if you consistently operate in the red. Not keeping proper accounts through separation of business and personal resources will lead to a fuzzy picture of your business' finances. You will be unable to tell if your organization is making or losing money.

Lack of Professionalism

Customers or clients writing checks using their name as opposed to the entity's name puts the validity of the business venture in question. It is advisable to take this aspect seriously, even if your business is part-time and/or you operate out of your home.

Missed Deductions

Comingling your business banking with your personal banking leads to a confusing mix of transactions on your bank account statement. The worst part about this is how easy it is to overlook deductions you might be entitled to. Regardless of who prepares your tax returns, sloppy recordkeeping is going to cost you time, money, and eventually missed deductions.

Limited Audit Trail

The United States government does not require you to have any specific recordkeeping method or even a separate bank account for that matter. Nonetheless, it does require that whatever procedure you use, all records are accurate, permanent, and show a clear record of income as well as deductions. Providing separate business statements along with records is going to present a clear audit trail.

How Can You Correct Commingling of Funds in an LLC?

Maybe you have already established your LLC and made the mistake of commingling funds. Recognizing this error early on in the process makes it easier to fix. To get started, you must identify all the transactions which were personal. Some of the most common expenses which are high up on the IRS' radar include travel, entertainment, meals, vehicles, and home office expenses.

Expenditures that ought to be personal can be reclassified. They could be changed to a fringe benefit compensation, distribution (draw) and/or a loan to the stakeholder. The funds that an investor disburses could be trickier to handle and might require the help of an accounting professional.

To summarize, commingling funds is going to cause a legal problem and a tax problem. The primary reason for forming an LLC in the first place is to decrease the owner's liability risks.

Chapter 9: Understanding and Navigating the Tax Landscape

"...but in this world, nothing can be said to be certain, except death and taxes." Benjamin Franklin (Statesman and one of the founding fathers of the USA)

The most common business structures which small business owners usually establish are a sole proprietorship, partnership, Limited Liability Company (LLC), S corporation or C Corporation. The structure you choose impacts your business' ability to raise money, determine taxes, and the consequences it might face when sued.

A limited liability company (LLC) is one of the legal entities which is formed under the state law. It offers some of the advantages of a corporation (for instance limited liability) but is comparatively easier to form as well as operate. Whenever a business entity is developed, it automatically receives a form of tax treatment by default.

A multi-member LLC is by default taxed as a partnership, whereas LLCs with only one owner are taxed as sole proprietorships which are essentially singly owned businesses. Nonetheless, LLCs might choose to be taxed as a C Corp or an S Corp. This can be accomplished by filling a document known as an "election" with the IRS. Once this is successfully done from the IRS' standpoint, the LLC is the same as a corporation and it files the tax forms required for that kind of entity. The following chapter provides a general overview on how current tax law affects specific entities. An in-depth analysis of tax consequences is beyond the scope of this book.

The Basics of Tax Law for LLCs

First, it is important to understand how an LLC is structured according to tax law. Unlike a corporation, LLCs are not taxed as separate business entities. Instead, all profits and losses "pass through" the business to each member of the LLC. LLC members report profits as well as losses on their personal federal tax returns, just like the owners of a partnership. The business does not pay federal income taxes, although some states do apply an annual tax to LLCs.

Depending on the number of members in your LLC, the IRS is going to treat your business as a sole proprietorship or partnership. Nonetheless, certain LLCs are by design classified as well as taxed as corporations by federal tax law. LLCs which are not automatically classified as corporations can select their business entity classification. To do so, an LLC must file Form 8832 (Form 2553 for S Corporation).

Income Taxes for Single Member LLCs

If you operate a single member LLC, the IRS is going to treat your business as a sole proprietorship (until and unless you choose to be a corporation), which means that the LLC itself does not pay taxes. You report all profits along with losses of the LLC on your personal income tax return (on a Schedule C) and file it with your 1040 tax return. You will also pay self-employment taxes on the entity's profits.

Income Taxes for Multi-Member LLCs

If your business has several owners, the IRS is going to treat your business as a partnership, unless you elect to be taxed as a corporation. As with sole proprietorships, the business does not pay taxes. Each owner is taxed on their share of the profits through their personal tax returns. How a multi-member LLC shares profits is defined in the LLC Operating Agreement. Even though it is not required by law in most states, this agreement is the one which structures your LLC's financial decisions, including how profits and losses are distributed.

You will also need to file Form 1065 (as all partnerships do) with the IRS. This form enables the IRS to determine if each member is reporting their income correctly. The LLC should also give each partner a Schedule K-1 showing each member's pro rata share of partnership income, credits, and deductions. Each member then reports this on their individual Form 1040 and Schedule E. If the LLC is a C- corporation or S Corporation, it should file Form 1120 and 1120S respectively.

If your LLC splits profits and losses in a manner that does not match each member's percentage interests, you should also request a "special allocation" from the IRS – something you ought to consult about with a CPA or tax attorney.

Paying Estimated Taxes

LLC owners and members are self-employed and therefore are not subject to tax withholding. Each member is advised to make a provision for self-employment taxes (Medicare and Social Security) quarterly to the IRS and their state tax agency.

If you have a multi-member LLC with an owner not actively involved in the LLC (*i.e.* they invested in the business but do not participate either through providing services or making management decisions), then that owner might be exempted from paying self-employment taxes. Your accountant or tax lawyer can tell you if your business meets the specific requirements of this exemption.

Employee Classification

Employee misclassification within small businesses is a bigger problem than some may think. Some companies classify employees as independent contractors to save money on payroll taxes. If a business pays an employee as a contractor through a 1099 form for miscellaneous income, the government can decide to reclassify individuals as meeting the criteria of employees and assess penalties and interest on back taxes.

Such situations can be very problematic whenever a contractor files for unemployment after losing their contract "job" and the state government has no record of employment on file. Although it could be tempting to do this to avoid paying payroll taxes for full-time employees, it is not worth the risk. Even with the protection of being incorporated, the government can still come after your personal assets if you try to dodge payroll taxes through misclassifications.

Sales Tax
Sales tax is a point of purchase tax imposed by state and local governments. The purchaser pays it and, as a small business owner, you assess it, collect it, and pass it on to the appropriate authorities within the prescribed time. Rates and laws vary from state to state, which often leads to confusion, especially if you sell to consumers in more than one state.

State Taxes
If you operate an LLC, you will typically pay taxes to your state in the same way you do to the IRS, through your individual returns. Some states charge an annual LLC fee, unrelated to income, also known as a franchise tax, registration fee, or renewal fee. It is a good idea to check the tax and business law in your state before you form an LLC.

In conclusion, knowing all the different types of taxes your small business is exposed to is equally as important as striving to maximize your organizational wealth. Horror stories exist of entrepreneurs who conceived and developed excellent products or services but lost everything within a short time because they failed to "render unto Caesar what was Caesar's."

Final Thoughts

As cliché as it might sound, the United States is a land of opportunities where success abounds for those who go after it. Regardless of the myriad of chances to succeed in the free economy, every budding entrepreneur will have to put in the necessary work upfront to be able to enjoy a piece of the cake down the road. According to the legendary football coach Vince Lombardi, "the dictionary is the only place that success comes before work."

Building a successful business is like growing a Chinese Bamboo Tree, as described in a well-known parable. It starts with planting, fertilizing, and constantly cultivating the seed by watering and fertilizing. Nothing comes out of the ground for five years, but the planter still must continue nurturing. If he/she neglects these chores at any time within those five years, all his/her labor would have been in vain. In year five, the first signs of the planter's hard work come to life as the tree gradually comes out of the soil. Five weeks later, the tree can grow to ninety feet.

The question to ask yourself is if the tree grew ninety feet in five years or five weeks. Obviously, the answer is five years because every life endeavor requires perseverance, hard work, faith, commitment, and never backing down when failure rears its ugly head - as it will. I think this story is analogous to growing a successful business. You might not see results for a long time, but you need to believe in your dreams, have measurable goals and work towards them endlessly.

Many people will find it ludicrous to work on a goal for five years without any results and some might even go as far as ridiculing the one who is obsessed with accomplishing his/her lifelong vision. The tree grows underground and develops a strong unshakeable foundation. In my opinion, the main reason most small businesses fail within five years is that their founders don't learn any lessons from the Chinese Bamboo Tree.

Bibliography

h.-2. -S. (n.d.).

h.-2. -L. (n.d.).

http://fortune.com/. (n.d.).

http://jbepnet.com/journals/Vol_3_No_1_March_2016/8.pdf. (n.d.).

http://psycnet.apa.org/record/1986-29994-001. (n.d.).

http://psycnet.apa.org/record/1998-01190-014. (n.d.).

http://www.academia.edu/. (n.d.).

http://www.aca-demia.edu/6415657/A_STUDY_ON_USE_OF_NON_MONE-TARY_INCENTIVES_AS_A_MOTIVA-TIONAL_TOOL_IN_THE_MANUFACTURING_SECTOR. (n.d.).

http://www.aca-demia.edu/6415657/A_STUDY_ON_USE_OF_NON_MONE-TARY_INCENTIVES_AS_A_MOTIVA-TIONAL_TOOL_IN_THE_MANUFACTURING_SECTOR. (n.d.).

http://www.vitaver.com/blog/2010/07/6-non-monetary-rewards-that-motivate-employees/. (n.d.).

https://dl.acm.org/citation.cfm?id=982403. (n.d.).

https://hbr.org/2011/05/the-power-of-small-wins. (n.d.).

https://iims.uthscsa.edu/sites/iims/files/Relationships-6.pdf. (n.d.).

https://taxfoundation.org/us-has-more-individually-owned-busi-nesses-corporations. (n.d.).

https://wol.iza.org/articles/goal-setting-and-worker-motivation/long. (n.d.).

https://www.lynda.com/Web-Design-tutorials/LLC-Advantages-disadvantages/163952/184252-4.html

https://www.entrepreneur.com/article/187366. (n.d.).

https://www.jstor.org/stable/4166134?seq=1#page_scan_tab_contents. (n.d.).

www.sba.gov/. (n.d.).

https://www.shrm.org/hr-today/trends-and-forecasting/research-and-surveys/Documents/2016-Employee-Job-Satisfaction-and-Engagement-Report.pdf. (n.d.).

https://www.shrm.org/hr-today/trends-and-forecasting/research-and-surveys/Documents/2016-Employee-Job-Satisfaction-and-Engagement-Report.pdf. (n.d.).

https://www.topechelon.com/blog/recruiter-training/sources-recruitment-types/

Edwin Locke: *Toward a Theory of Task Motivation and Incentives* (Locke, 1968)

(https://wol.iza.org/articles/goal-setting-and-worker-motivation/long)

(http://jbepnet.com/journals/Vol_3_No_1_March_2016/8.pdf)

(http://psycnet.apa.org/record/1986-29994-001) Tubbs, 1996

Mento, Steel, & Karren, 1987; Phillips & Gully, 1997;

Tubbs, 1986; Yukl & Latham, 1978.

(Kerr & Landauer, 2004) (https://www.jstor.org/stable/4166134?seq=1#page_scan_tab_contents).

(Latham, 2004; Latham & Locke, 2006

(Seijts & Latham, 2005)

(Donovan & Radosevich, 1998; Klein et al., 1999; Wofford, Goodwin, & Premack, 1993)

(Shaw, 2004) (https://dl.acm.org/citation.cfm?id=982403)

www.ingramcontent.com/pod-product-compliance
Lightning Source LLC
Chambersburg PA
CBHW041104180526
45172CB00001B/104